Really Short Walks
East Devon Coast

Robert Hesketh

Bossiney Books

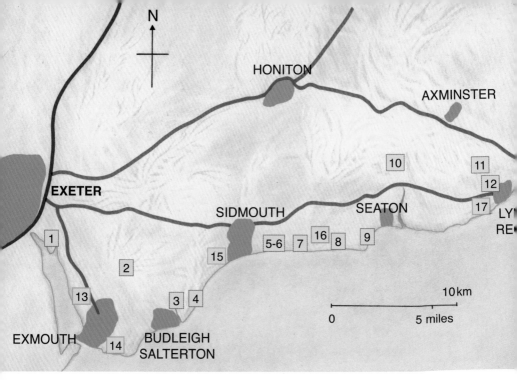

The approximate locations of the walks in this book
(there-and-back walks in red-framed boxes)

All the walks in this book were checked prior to publication, at
which time the instructions were correct. However, changes can
occur in the countryside over which neither the author nor
the publisher has any control. Please let us know
if you encounter any serious problems.

First published 2011 by Bossiney Books Ltd,
33 Queens Drive, Ilkley, LS29 9QW
www.bossineybooks.com

© 2011 Robert Hesketh All rights reserved
ISBN 978-1-906474-29-4

Acknowledgements
The maps are by Nick Hawken.
Cover based on a design by Heards Design Partnership.
All photographs are by the author or from the publisher's own collection.

Printed in Great Britain by R Booth Ltd, Penryn, Cornwall

Introduction

The walks in this book are mostly 3-5km (2-3 miles) in length. Some are easy, others short but challenging. All have been chosen to show east Devon's unparalleled scenery – cliffs and beaches, woodland, waterfalls and rivers – except one: we've cheated and included a lovely walk at Lyme Regis, where all but a hundred metres of the route is just over the border in Dorset.

We have not suggested how long they will take, because these routes offer many wonderful viewpoints and places of interest to linger over – and some people walk faster than others.

Clothing and footwear

Do go prepared. Devon's weather can change rapidly, and even within a short walk there may be a considerable temperature difference when you climb from a sheltered valley to a cliff top exposed to a sea breeze. Always carry extra layers of clothing as well as a waterproof.

On some paths, especially inland, you are likely to come across briars, thorns and nettles, so bare legs can be a liability. There will be some mud at most times of the year and perhaps a lot of mud and puddles in winter and after a wet spell. Ideally, therefore, wear walking boots – and certainly not sandals! Wellington boots are not recommended, as they don't breathe or provide ankle support. I find a walking pole is a considerable help. Finally, carry water, as dehydration causes tiredness.

Safety

Please watch out for uneven ground, especially on the Coast Path and keep clear of the cliff edge because it is not fenced off from the drop. Take special care when the path does take you near the edge, especially if there are signs of crumbling or erosion. Go no nearer than you have to and keep a close eye on children and dogs. The sketch maps in this book are just that – sketches. You may want to carry an OS Explorer map for extra information.

The countryside

Despite many pressures on their livelihoods, farmers are still trying to make a living from the land you will pass through. Please respect their crops. Leave gates closed or open as you find them, and keep dogs under control, especially during the lambing and bird nesting season.

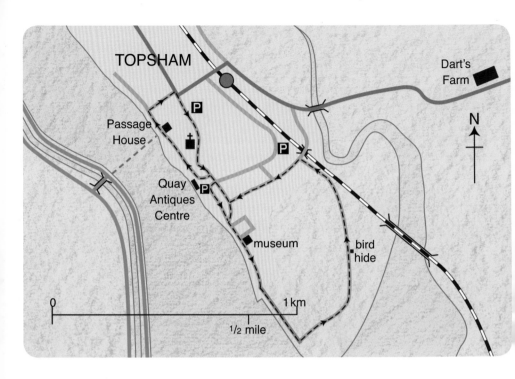

Walk 1   Topsham

Distance: 3.3km
Character: This well surfaced, mainly level walk can be completed in
an hour, but deserves longer. The riverside settlement of Topsham has
charm and character and retains a wealth of historic buildings, mainly
from 1660-1730, the period of its greatest prosperity. Take binoculars, as
there are excellent bird watching opportunities, especially in winter.

From the central car park, turn left into Fore Street (or use alternative
parking in Holman Way or on the Quay if this is full). Walk past the
Salutation, a classic coaching inn with a splendid Georgian façade.
Continue past the church with its red sandstone tower and the Globe
Hotel which, like the Salutation, has a Georgian façade hiding what is
almost certainly a much older building.

Follow Fore Street as far as the Lighter Inn, named after the barges
that carried goods on to Exeter. On the Quay is the cast iron King's
Beam, formerly used to weigh dutiable goods.

Continue ahead (signed MUSEUM) into the Strand, passing the magnificent Shell House of 1571. Number 25, one of the Strand's late 17th
century merchants' houses, is now Topsham Museum.

Continue down the Strand with its Dutch-gabled houses. Topsham ships trading with the Netherlands brought back Dutch building styles and small Dutch bricks in ballast to create one of Devon's most unusual and attractive streets.

At the end of the Strand continue ahead, following the raised bankside GOAT WALK. At low tide, flocks of waders and gulls commonly feed on the exposed mud.

At the end of the Goat Walk, bear left into a tarred lane. Continue past houses. A pair of iron gates on the right leads to a bird-watching platform about 130 m away. Continue for a further 300 m where there is an RSPB bird-watching hide beside the road. Overlooking Bowling Green Marsh, it contains a wealth of information about birds.

Continue along the lane. Follow it uphill when it bends left at the railway. Turn first left into MONMOUTH STREET, which has several fine houses. At the far end of Monmouth Street, turn right along Monmouth Hill. At the end of Monmouth Hill, walk ahead into FORE STREET then almost immediately turn left into FERRY ROAD, which runs parallel to the river. Ferry Road has many historic houses with maritime connections, including the Passage House Inn next to the foot ferry. Continue along Ferry Road. Reaching Follett Road, turn right and right again into Fore Street. Continue to the car park.

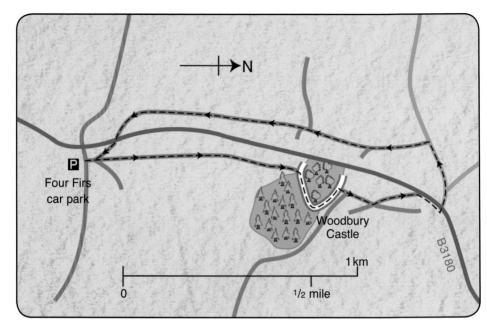

Walk 2   Woodbury Castle

Distance: 3.5km (2 miles)
Character: An easy walk in the distinctive heathland of Woodbury
Common, taking in Woodbury Castle, one of Devon's most impressive
pre-Roman hill forts.

Start from the Four Firs car park (SY 032864). To get there, follow the B3180 southward from A3052. Turn left signed YETTINGTON/EAST BUDLEIGH, and immediately turn right into the car park.

Cross the lane from the car park and take the path ahead, marked with the pink EAST DEVON WAY arrow. Then take the middle path of three and walk gently uphill, parallel to the main road, towards a large clump of trees which conceals Woodbury Castle.

Woodbury Castle
Commanding good views all round, Woodbury Castle would have been kept clear of trees when it was occupied, between 500 and 300 BC. Its circular ramparts – still of considerable height despite erosion – were once topped with wooden palisades. A refuge in times of danger, it also sheltered a permanent settlement of wooden houses, probably centred on the hall of a local chief.

Cross its car park and continue up steps to the rim of the inner bank, which would have had a palisade. Either walk across the central area, or follow the bank anticlockwise, but if you do, watch out for tree roots, and avoid scrambling on the bank sides, which erode easily.

Leave the Castle on the north side and find a path out of the wood. A broad path runs round the perimeter of the wood, then heads north, parallel to the main road. Join this path.

At a path crossing, bear left (PUBLIC BRIDLEWAY) and cross rough ground to another bridleway fingerpost by the road. Turn right alongside the road for 100 m to a junction. Cross the main road carefully, and turn left, WOODBURY.

Follow the lane for 350 m then turn left, PUBLIC BRIDLEWAY (EAST DEVON WAY). Ignore side turnings and continue for 1.3 km to the B3180. Cross onto a minor path, which leads back to the car park.

Pebblebed heaths

Woodbury Common is the largest of East Devon's 'pebblebed heaths', characterised by heather, gorse and birch. Agricultural intensification, combined with land-take for road and house building, have made heathland an increasingly rare and threatened habitat of great conservation value. Woodbury is a Site of Special Scientific Interest and its fauna includes significant populations of Dartford warblers and nightjars.

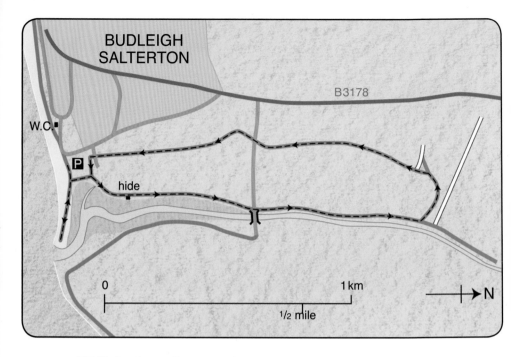

Walk 3   Otter Estuary circuit

Distance: 5.25 km (3¹/₄ miles)

Character: From Budleigh's pebble beach, this easy and level walk follows a pretty riverbank path beside the Otter Estuary Nature Reserve. Take binoculars: large flocks of waders and gulls are often seen, especially in winter. The return section by quiet paths and tracks can be muddy, so after very wet weather you might prefer to make it a there-and-back walk.

Start by walking from Budleigh Salterton's Lime Kiln car park to the far end of the beach to enjoy the views of the Otter estuary. In medieval times, before the pebble ridge formed, the Otter was navigable as far as Otterton. The saltpans (hence Budleigh Salterton) were worked where the bird-rich mudflats are now.

Retrace your steps to the near end of the car park. Turn right COAST PATH LADRAM BAY. Continue on the same path (LADRAM BAY) at the next signpost. The path follows the old sea wall built by prisoners of war in Napoleonic times. There are bird-watching points and a hide further along on the right.

Reaching the road bridge, continue upriver on the bankside path for 900 m. Fork left (BUDLEIGH SALTERTON) when the path divides.

8

This path diverges from the river on a raised embankment with an aqueduct on the right.

Follow the path in a gentle half circle. When it starts to curve right, turn left over a stile. Cross the next stile and continue along the broad and sometimes muddy track. Continue when this narrows to a path.

Meeting a lane, continue through a kissing gate, PUBLIC FOOTPATH BUDLEIGH SALTERTON. When you reach the next lane, cross and bear left past a play park and then turn right to the car park.

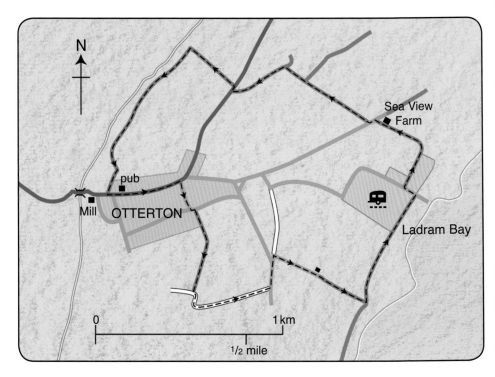

Walk 4   Otterton and Ladram Bay

Distance: 5.3km (3¹/₄ miles)
Character: A delightfully varied walk with coast path, field paths and
a riverbank section, as well as a picturesque village and spectacular
views along the Jurassic Coast.

Park carefully in Otterton's Fore Street, near the Mill. Walk east past
the King's Arms, following the leat upstream past typically West
Country 16th and 17th century thatched cottages with external chimney stacks and garden walls built with local flints.

At the top of Fore Street, turn right into LEA ROAD. At the end of Lea
Road, turn left at the T-junction then almost immediately right into
an unsigned path. After 450m join a farm track, which soon takes a
90° left turn.

At the end of the track turn left along a lane. After 100m, fork right
and almost immediately turn right along a narrow lane, which ends
at a house. Continue ahead, PUBLIC FOOTPATH, to a kissing gate, then
along the field with the hedge on your right.

Turn left at the end of the field, COAST PATH LADRAM BAY. The
impressive succession of cliffs ahead begins with Ladram Bay and its

10

red sandstone seastacks. Peak Hill is next, with Sidmouth beyond. The line continues past the white chalk of Beer Head to Golden Cap, with Chesil Beach and Portland Bill in the far distance.

At the far end of the field continue on CLIFF TOP ROUTE PROVIDED BY LADRAM BAY CARAVAN PARK. At the end of the next field follow the short path ahead down to a lane. Leave the coast path here, turning left, then after 20m (just before the telephone booths, café and take-away) turn right along a track.

After 200m it turns 90° left, and climbs to Sea View Farm. Turn left along the lane. Then, after just 30m, turn right (COUNTY ROAD) along a green track. After 400m, keep left at a junction, then at a T-junction of paths turn left, COUNTY ROAD.

When you reach the lane, turn right and almost immediately left, PUBLIC RIGHT OF WAY (RYDON LANE). Beside an open barn, continue ahead then downhill to the river. Turn left up four steps to a kissing gate. Follow the path through fields, parallel to the river, then go through a kissing gate and down an enclosed path into Otterton.

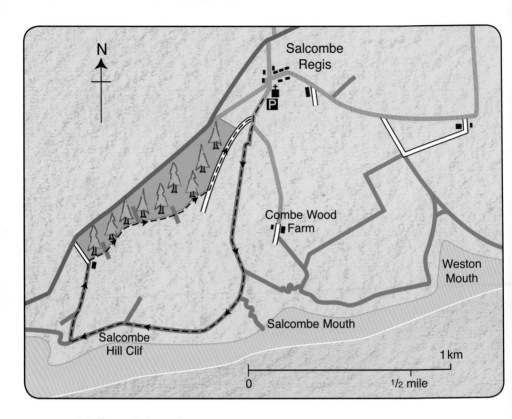

Walk 5 Salcombe Regis West

Distance: 3.6km (2¹/₄ miles)
Character: This is rather more demanding than the adjacent Walk 6,
but the effort of climbing Salcombe Hill Cliff is richly rewarded by
stunning views east to Portland Bill and west to Torbay.

Start from Salcombe Regis church car park, SY148888 (contributions
requested). Turn left down the lane. Ignore the first footpath right and
take the second, just 30m further on, PUBLIC FOOTPATH SALCOMBE
MOUTH AND COAST PATH.

After about 50m, bear right through a kissing gate as signed. Follow
the path downhill through fields to a bridge and fingerpost. Continue
ahead, COAST PATH SALCOMBE MOUTH SIDMOUTH.

If you wish to visit Salcombe Mouth, divert left after another
200m down a steep path as signed. Otherwise continue, COAST PATH
SIDMOUTH. At first the path rises gently over the sandstone, but the
gradient increases sharply when it reaches the greensand, chalk and
flints which cap the cliff. Rest on the bench halfway up and look back

12

to Higher Dunscombe Cliff, a similar formation with reddish sandstone at the base and creamy coloured greensand above.

A second bench stands at the summit of Salcombe Hill Cliff, 120 m above sea level. Ignore the footpath right and continue on the coast path to the next fingerpost. Turn right, SALCOMBE HILL CAR PARK, but before you do so walk ahead another 50 m to the viewing table. Sidmouth lies below, with the sandstone cliffs beyond. The first of these is High Peak, an impressive 157 m.

Return to the fingerpost and turn inland on a gravel path. Ignore side turnings and pass a house, then turn right across its drive and follow the footpath through conifers. Cross a farm track and continue along the inside edge of the plantation to a path crossing.

Continue ahead, SALCOMBE REGIS, steeply downhill to a track. Again, continue ahead, PUBLIC FOOTPATH, which will bring you to a lane. Turn left, back up to the car park.

'Salt Valley'

Salcombe Regis shelters in a warm south-facing valley and derives its name (as does the bigger Salcombe in the South Hams) from 'salt valley'. Salt production from seawater must have been an ancient trade, as the settlement was recorded as Sealt Cumbe in 1050, but Regis ('of the king') was not added till the 18th century.

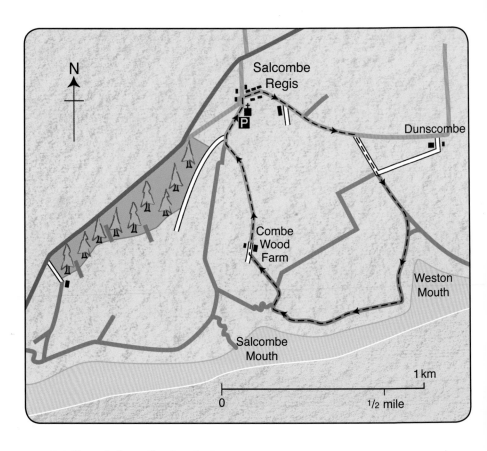

Walk 6 Salcombe Regis East

Distance: 3.3km (2 miles)
*Character: An inland section on quiet lanes and footpaths leads to a
cliff top walk with splendid views of the Jurassic Coast. There are two
short ascents and a longer descent, part of which may be tricky in
muddy conditions. This walk could be combined with Walk 5.*

From Salcombe Regis church car park, SY148888 (contributions
requested), turn right uphill on the lane. Pass the church and turn
right again, passing stone and thatch cottages, then climbing steadily
up the lane.

At the top of the hill turn right on a farm track, PUBLIC FOOTPATH
LINCOMBE AND COAST PATH. When this track makes a left turn,
continue ahead on a grassy track, PUBLIC FOOTPATH. When the path
divides, bear right to a gate and over a stile. At the fingerpost ahead,
keep right, COAST PATH SALCOMBE MOUTH.

14

Follow the coast path until it starts to descend, and turns sharp right. After 20 m, leave the coast path and continue inland, PUBLIC FOOTPATH SALCOMBE REGIS AND DUNSCOMBE. After 40 m the path again divides. This time bear left and downhill. Continue downhill at the next footpath sign.

At the foot of the descent, bear right onto the farm track through Combe Wood Farm. It soon becomes a lane leading back to the church.

> **Salcombe Regis Church**
> Built of locally quarried greensand – a superb building stone used extensively in Exeter Cathedral – the church is noted for its fragments of Norman work (piers and capitals) and its 15th century tower. Also 15th century is a wooden lectern. The beautiful engraved glass triptych above the altar was designed by Laurence Whistler.

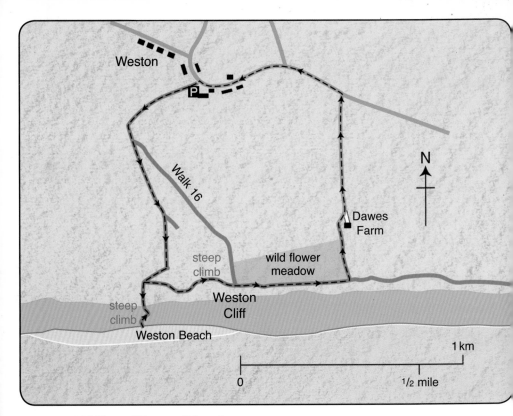

Walk 7   Weston Mouth

Distance: 4.3km (2³/₄ miles)
*Character: This tough but rewarding walk involves one long descent
and a long, steep ascent. You can make it much easier and shorter
using the path described in Walk 16. Choose a clear morning to enjoy
the superb westerly views. Out of season you might have this rarely
visited corner of the coast to yourself. Please note (especially if you
want a swim) that Weston is a nudist beach.*

Start from the small car park near Lower Weston Farm (SY 166890)
indicated by a sign PUBLIC FOOTPATH WESTON MOUTH AND COAST-
PATH. Walk downhill through a gate into the enclosed path, which
descends Weston Combe.

At the National Trust WESTON MOUTH sign, turn right across a
field to a kissing gate, where there is an information board about the
Combe. It is another 250m to the beach laterally, and 45m vertically.
Fortunately there are steps.

Return to the kissing gate and bear right, COASTPATH BRANSCOMBE

16

MOUTH, beginning a long climb up Weston Cliff to the welcome bench at the top, and superlative views. (The inland path here is that used in Walk 16.) Continue east on the coast path. Either follow the clifftop path or divert left after a few metres into a wild flower meadow, rich with cowslips in spring and butterflies in summer, and walk parallel to the coast path.

At the end of the field turn left beside an information board describing local fauna and flora, PUBLIC FOOTPATH DAWES AND WESTON.

Continue with the hedge on your right, over two stiles and into a track. Continue past Dawes Farm and along a tarmac track. At the lane, turn left, and keep left at the next junction, back to the car park.

Smuggling in East Devon

The Revenue men who kept watch at Weston Mouth lookout during the 18th and early 19th centuries had a lonely task. East Devon was notorious for smuggling. It had plenty of fishermen and coastwise traders who knew the local waters and secluded beaches better than anyone. Such men also knew routes to the Channel Islands and France, chief sources of contraband brandy and tobacco. East Devon smugglers enjoyed almost unanimous support from the local community, usually including the Establishment of magistrates, clergy and gentry.

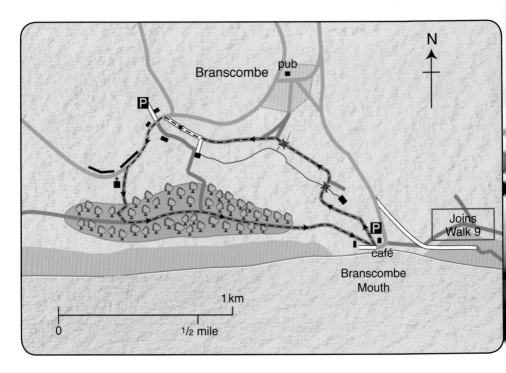

Walk 8   Branscombe

Distance: 3.1 km (2 miles)
*Character: As well as splendid coastal views, this short walk has a
great deal of interest: a historic church, England's only thatched forge,
Devon's last traditional bakery (which also offers teas) and a working
watermill. There is one steepish ascent and one steep descent.*

Start at Branscombe's Village Hall car park (donations requested) – or
head east through the village and turn right to park at Branscombe
Mouth if this is full.

From the Village Hall, turn right past the forge, where blacksmiths
can be seen practising their craft. Like the bakery and watermill, the
forge is open to the public and under the care of the National Trust.

Follow the lane uphill. Bear left (PUBLIC FOOTPATH) into the
churchyard, and left again (PUBLIC FOOTPATH) in the churchyard.

Leave the churchyard by a stile and footbridge. Follow the path
uphill through a field and over another stile into woodland. The path
climbs steeply with steps. Turn left (COAST PATH). This is level at first,
before descending sharply, relieved in parts by steps. A fabulous view
of Branscombe Mouth and Hooken Undercliff opens out.

At the foot of the slope turn left by the fingerpost BRANSCOMBE VILLAGE – or divert onto the beach to enjoy the view, visit the shop, café or toilets and see the information boards. These explain something of the local geology and the story of MSC *Napoli*, wrecked at Branscombe Mouth in 2007. *Napoli's* 14 tonne anchor lies nearby as a memorial.

Return to the fingerpost and follow the level, well-surfaced path. Keep left, BRANSCOMBE VILLAGE. At the second footbridge, either divert right for refreshment at the Mason's Arms, or continue ahead towards Branscombe.

On reaching Manor Mill either continue on the tarred track, BRANSCOMBE, which leads back to the Village Hall, or divert left to visit the mill. From the mill, follow the field path on to the bakery, where the traditional wood oven and baking equipment, which were still in regular use until 1987, have been preserved. There is also a fascinating small museum of local life, with tableaux and oral history recordings.

> You could make a full day out by combining this walk with the more strenuous Walk 9, perhaps lunching at the Mason's Arms, the Bakery, or the Fountain Inn at the west end of Branscombe.

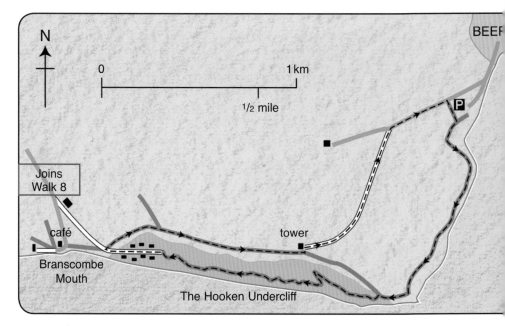

Walk 9   Beer

Distance: 5km (3 miles)
*Character: As well as giving superb views from Beer Head, this walk
passes through the extraordinary Hooken Undercliff. There is one
seriously tough ascent, and one steep descent which some people may
find vertiginous.*

Start from Beer's Cliff Top car park (SY 228888). Facing the sea, turn
right, COAST PATH BRANSCOMBE MOUTH, and continue to Beer Head,
England's most westerly chalk headland, with its distinctive rock pin-
nacles. Enjoy the view across Seaton Bay and along the Dorset coast
to Portland Bill, before turning west.

The Hooken Undercliff

Like the more extensive undercliffs between Axmouth and Lyme
Regis, this was created by a landslip, and has vegetation and a
sheltered micro-climate quite different from the breezy cliffs
above. The landslip occurred one night in 1790, when heavy rain
caused the top layer of chalk and greensand to slide over the layer
of clay which separated it from the Lias below. Four hectares of
land slipped 60 m down and 200 m seaward.

When the Coast Path divides, turn left through a kissing gate (COAST PATH BRANSCOMBE MOUTH). Follow this Undercliff path downhill and then along below the cliffs for 1.5 km. Look up to watch the birds of prey wheeling above, or screaming gulls nesting. The colours of the cliffs indicate the various rocks of which they are composed, in a cross-section of geological time: the white chalk overlies the more ancient golden Lias.

When you reach a mobile home park, continue ahead on a track (BRANSCOMBE MOUTH) to the entrance gate. Turn sharp right, PUBLIC FOOTPATH HOOKEN CLIFFS BEER.

It's a steep climb, relieved in part by steps, but the view from the bench at the top is magnificent. The path is nearly level from here, along the top of the cliffs.

Just beyond a tower (the old Coastguard lookout) bear left, PUBLIC BRIDLEWAY. Join the chalk track from the tower. Cross a cattle grid and continue to a tarmac lane. Follow it downhill to the car park.

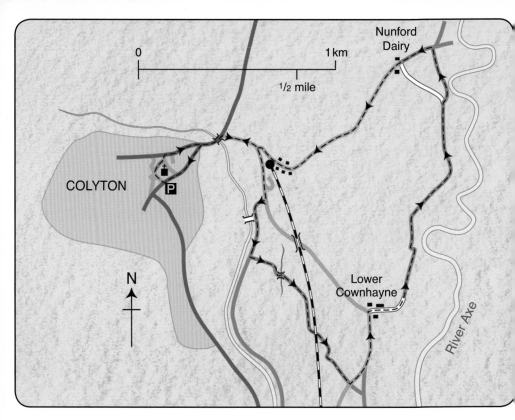

Walk 10   Colyton

Distance: 4.8km (3 miles) from the tram station (take the tram from Seaton) or 6.3km (4 miles) from the town centre car park
Character: A gentle walk by meadows and lanes. Parts of the walk may be very wet, so boots are vital.

From the Colyton tram station: Walk through the car park on the western side of the track, and down to the road. Turn left and follow the directions as from the * below.

From the Dolphin Street car park in Colyton: Walk up the lane opposite the car park into the town square, past Old Church House (1612) with its stained glass windows on your right. At the church, bear right on the footpath curving around the churchyard.

At the end of the footpath, turn left and almost immediately right by the Gerard Arms, signed TRAMWAY. Continue ahead at the next two junctions, cross the bridge and turn right, TRAMWAY STATION.

Ignore both a lane on the left and the entrance to the station car park*. After another 130m, turn right through a metal kissing gate

and follow the riverbank path left, past the footbridge to the end of the field. Turn left (EAST DEVON WAY) and keep the fence on your right.

Turn right through a metal gate and almost immediately left over a footbridge. Follow the path diagonally right over the next field, and leave by a ladder stile in the far corner. Cross the tramline with care. Continue diagonally right across a field, then along the right edge of the next, larger, field, to a lane.

Ignore the footpath opposite and turn left and follow the lane for 400 m, to a farm. Turn right (PUBLIC FOOTPATH) between farm buildings and follow the track to a kissing gate. Continue ahead (EAST DEVON WAY) with the hedge on your left and leave the field at the far end by a stile. Continue with the hedge on your right, then turn right over another stile.

Cut diagonally across the next field as signed and follow the EAST DEVON WAY upriver, as far as a kissing gate at the foot of a farm track. Don't follow the track. Turn right and follow the edge of the field. (If there's an electric fence, there should be a plastic handle to unclip and let you through.)

Follow the bankside path. Arriving at a cross track, turn left uphill and pass Nunford Dairy. Continue up the lane ahead to the summit and then down to Colyton tram station.

Follow the lane downhill and turn right, TOWN CENTRE. Turn left over the bridge, then keep left up DOLPHIN STREET to the car park.

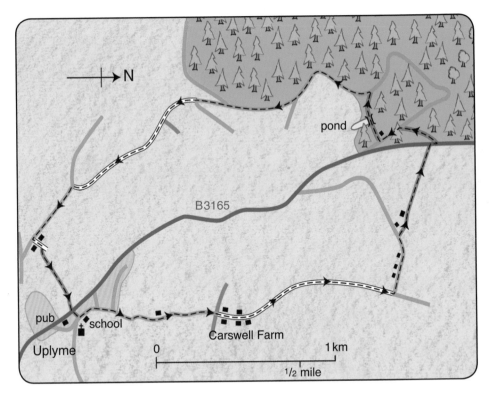

Walk 11   Uplyme

Distance: 5.8km (3¹/₂ miles)
Character: A mixture of woodland, field paths and quiet lanes,
exploring the green hilly landscape on the Dorset border. Expect mud
in places. Some paths may be overgrown, so long trousers are
advisable. Although not strenuous, it does include one long steady
ascent at the beginning.

Park considerately on the road near the church. Facing the church,
turn left and follow the road downhill past the school. Turn right after
200m into LIME KILN LANE and 40m ahead turn right again, PUBLIC
BRIDLEWAY.

This tarmac track climbs steadily past a footpath junction and
through Carswell Farm. Follow it between farm buildings and continue
till you reach a tarmac lane. Turn left and follow the lane for 250m.
Just after it bends left, turn right through a gate, PUBLIC BRIDLEWAY.

At first enclosed, the bridleway then leads downhill with a hedge on
the left through three fields, separated by gates, to a road. Turn right

and follow the road for 40 m. Cross with care, turn left and follow a track (COUNTY ROAD) downhill through trees.

Turn left onto a lane. Walk past the entrance to a house. At the end of its garden, turn right down a short track towards a metal gate. Cross the stile on the right and follow the PUBLIC FOOTPATH downhill through trees. (Beware the ditch on the right!)

Cross a footbridge (there's a charming pond to the left) and follow the path uphill to another lane. Turn left. At a junction, keep right. At the next junction, fork left, CAT HOLE LANE. After 150 m the lane turns left: continue ahead (PUBLIC BRIDLEWAY) and pass gardens. Continue ahead on the bridleway at the next two path junctions.

On reaching a lane, there's a fine view of a railway viaduct, part of the now dismantled 1903 branch line from Axminster to Lyme Regis. Turn left down the lane and take the next turning left, between 'Beech House' and 'Gemini'. After 30 m, turn right, PUBLIC FOOTPATH.

Continue with the hedge on your left, then follow the edge of the cricket field to the main road. Cross carefully, and climb the steps opposite (PUBLIC FOOTPATH) back to the church, which has an ancient yew (possibly 1000 years old) in the churchyard.

For refreshments at the Talbot Arms, divert right down Church Street and continue for 250 m to the main road.

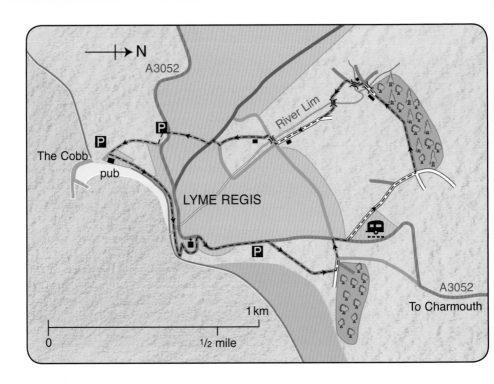

Walk 12 Lyme Regis

Distance: 5.3 km (3 1/4 miles)
Character: A circuit of Lyme Regis. Moderate ascents and descents.

Start from the Charmouth Road car park. Turn right and walk uphill. After 150 m, opposite the cemetery, bear right through a kissing gate (acorn sign). Cut diagonally across three fields, then turn left along a track. When the coast path turns off right, continue ahead down a lane to the main road.

Turn right and after 75 m bear left into a caravan park. Although not signed, this is a footpath. Follow the main driveway, which at the end of the park becomes a track.

Ignore a footpath to the left. At a junction, turn left on a footpath (LYME REGIS) and walk down fields, then onward down a track.

Cross a bridge and turn left (LYME REGIS). You are now briefly in Devon! Cross a footbridge and again turn left, down the valley. Follow first the path then a farm driveway till you reach a road. Turn right across the bridge, then left through a gateway into Slopes Farm. Almost immediately bear right on the waymarked footpath. Climb through woodland to a road, and turn right.

Approaching Uplyme Mill

The front at Lyme Regis

At a road junction, turn left and immediately right into POUND ROAD. Follow this to a junction with the Sidmouth Road. Cross it and head diagonally left across the car park, to a pedestrian exit into Cobb Road. Turn right and walk down to the Cobb.

You may well want to explore the Cobb area. If not, turn left at The Cobb Arms. When the street ends, continue along the promenade to the parking area by the clock tower. Lyme's main street, Broad Street, runs up to the left.

Continue along the sea front till you reach information boards with a view over the area of massive landslips known as the Spittles. Turn sharp left uphill, then sharp right, PUBLIC FOOTPATH ST MICHAEL'S CHURCH AND CHURCHYARD. Walk through the churchyard, then turn right up the main road to the car park.

Suggestions for there-and-back walks

Walk 13 Lympstone

This 2km walk on field paths includes good views of the Exe. It uses the East Devon Way to reach A La Ronde, a unique National Trust property with sixteen sides and an extensive shell collection. (Phone 01395 265514 to check opening hours.)

Turn left out of Underhill car park. Follow the No Through Road for 200m to a junction of paths. Turn right, PUBLIC FOOTPATH. Continue to a kissing gate. Follow the path for another 150m to a second kissing gate. Turn left, EAST DEVON WAY.

Reaching a lane, cross over. Cross a stile and follow the field path along the left field edge as signed and cross another stile. Turn right (EAST DEVON WAY) and follow the well beaten and signed path through a series of fields to a lane. Turn left, EAST DEVON WAY. Cross the main road carefully and follow SUMMER LANE for 200m to A La Ronde.

Walk 14 Exmouth

Park at the eastern end of Exmouth's sea front road – or at Foxholes car park if all roadside parking is taken. Follow the sea front to the far end, where a plaque proclaims 'World Heritage Site Entrance'. This is the start of the 'Jurassic Coast', which stretches east to Studland in Dorset.

Turn left (COAST PATH SANDY BAY BUDLEIGH SALTERTON) and follow the zigzag path uphill. Turn right. Divert right (RODNEY POINT) and continue to ORCOMBE POINT, which has splendid views, especially of the Exe estuary.

Walk 15 Peak Hill

A 500m level walk over the turf leads to extensive views both east and west along the coast (see photo above). Start from Peak Hill car park 1km west of Sidmouth (SY 110873). Cross the road with care and continue ahead, PUBLIC FOOTPATH LINK TO COAST PATH.

If you wish to explore the heath and woodland known as Mutter's Moor, north of the car park, consult the information board at the eastern end of the car park first to see the layout of paths – there are more paths on the ground than are shown on the Explorer map. Mutter's Moor is named after the smuggling family who used their legitimate wood and turf cutting business as a cover for transporting contraband. It is most attractive in summer when the gorse and later heather are in flower.

Walk 16   Weston Cliff and wildflower meadow

This is a route to give you the best views of Walk 7 without the same degree of exercise! In fact it's nearly flat, and about 2.5km there and back. The wildflower meadow is at its best in Spring. The view is fantastic at all times of year, but choose a bright morning if you can.

Start from the small car park near Lower Weston Farm (SY 166890) indicated by a sign PUBLIC FOOTPATH WESTON MOUTH AND COAST-PATH. Walk downhill through a gate into the enclosed path, which descends Weston Combe.

After 400 m, fork left on a track heading slightly uphill, and follow it out to the cliff, where there is a bench. If you turn left along the coast path, the entrance to the wildflower meadow is immediately on your left.

Walk 17　The Undercliff from Lyme Regis

Start from Holmbush car park on the western edge of Lyme Regis. Follow the COAST PATH sign at the southern end of the car park. At the path junction, turn left, TO COAST PATH. The path immediately divides. Bear left and downhill. Only 30 m ahead, turn right, COAST PATH SEATON. Great views east onto the Dorset cliffs open out.

Follow the Coast Path over turf and into the 304 hectare Axmouth-Lyme Regis Nature Reserve. An information board explains how landslips have created the undercliffs, where a variety of plants and animals thrive. Continue ahead for 1.5 km through dense woodland along the fairly level but uneven Coast Path to get a flavour of the undercliffs, eerily quiet apart from birdsong and the murmur of insects. Alternatively, branch right at the second information panel and climb steeply to Chimney Rock for an overview of the undercliffs – though dense foliage obscures this in summer.

31

By the same author

Shortish Walks in East Devon (5-10km)
Cob and Thatch – the inside story
The Devon Beach & Cove Guide
Devon's Geology
Devon's History
Devon Place Names
Devon Smugglers – the truth behind the fiction
Where to Watch Wildlife in Devon

Other 'really short walks' books

Really Short Walks North Cornwall
Really Short Walks North Dartmoor
Really Short Walks South Dartmoor
Really Short Walks North Devon
Really Short Walks South Devon

For a full list of our walks books please see our website
www.bossineybooks.com